"Never ask of money spent
Where the spender thinks it went.
Nobody was ever meant
To remember or invent
What he did with every cent."

—ROBERT FROST

How to carve **a bean**

"Hunger maketh hard beans sweete."
—Proverbs & Epigrams, 1867

1. Lay the bean, in this case a plump, mature Fordhook lima *(Phaseolus lunatus)*, on its side on a cutting board and grasp it firmly by the shoulder portion.

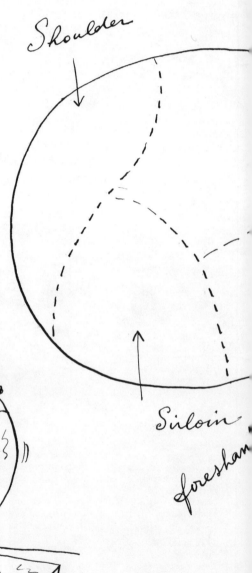

Shoulder

Sirloin

foreshank

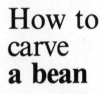

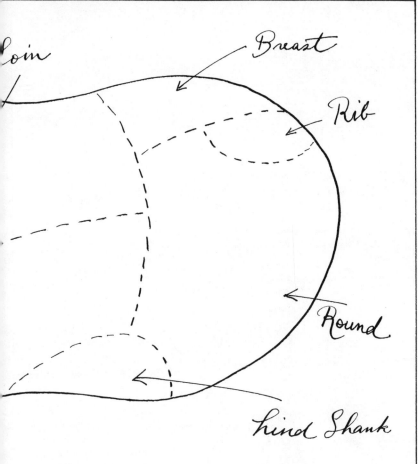

Loin

Breast

Rib

Round

hind Shank

2. Using a sharp knife, separate the fore-shank from the loin; this section, when roasted, makes a superb brisket.

3. Next trim away the tender hind shank cutlet, taking care, as always, to slice cleanly —NOT TEAR!—the lustrous skin.

4. Remove the sirloin and loin portions together, then separate them; the former is the meatiest and most tender section of the bean, whereas the adjacent rib is a trifle on the tough side.

5. The breast comes next (a special treat when braised).

6. Last, pare the round, leaving the succulent shoulder portion, which makes a robust broth.

All bean sections are best served piping hot, and reheated leftovers are nothing to sneeze at either. Enjoy!

N E E D E D !

Ph.D., M.B.A., M.P.A., D.N.S., L.P.N., M.S.W., M.D., C.P.A., M.F.A., B.F.A., M.S., B.S., B.A., D.D.S., B.S.E.E., B.M., M.S.C.S., LL.B., LL.D., M.A.L.S., F.B.A., O.T., Th.Ds., R.N., J.D., for key administrative post. We seek an assistant cook to prepare the alphabet soup served in municipal soup kitchens and on bread lines. Apply at City Hall, soonest.

SUDDENLY
POOR!

A GUIDE FOR THE DOWNWARDLY MOBILE

NOT FOR RESALE

TIMOTHY WHITE, J.C. SUARÈS & JUDY GARLAN

An Atlantic Monthly Press Book
Little, Brown and Company

BOSTON   TORONTO

"What our country needs is a good big laugh.
If someone could get off a good joke every ten
days, I think our troubles would be over."

—HERBERT HOOVER'S SUREFIRE CURE FOR
OVERNIGHT IMPOVERISHMENT, 1931

Credits and acknowledgements appear on page 96.

COPYRIGHT © 1983 BY TIMOTHY WHITE, J.C. SUARÈS, AND JUDY GARLAN

LIBRARY OF CONGRESS CATALOG CARD NO. 83-081239
FIRST EDITION
ISBN 0-316-93607-3

ATLANTIC-LITTLE, BROWN BOOKS
ARE PUBLISHED BY
LITTLE, BROWN AND COMPANY
IN ASSOCIATION WITH
THE ATLANTIC MONTHLY PRESS

BP

Published simultaneously in Canada
by Little, Brown & Company (Canada) Limited

PRINTED IN THE UNITED STATES OF AMERICA

Dedicated to the Pauper Nonpareil

No one is immune to criticism from the moneyed class.
According to the Omaha World Herald,
in 1973 the Melrose Drive Church of Christ in
Dallas, Texas, received a series of computer-typed
letters from a correspondence school, advertising
careers in electronics. One of the pushier of
the epistles stated: "Accept the challenge, Mr. Christ!
Don't waste your life in a dead-end,
low-paying job!"

C O N T E N T S

PAGE 11

PAGE 16

PAGE 76

PAGE 15

CONTENTS

PAGE 17

PAGE 61

PAGE 41

PAGE 84

PAGE 49

"Poverty in the United States is a culture,
an institution, a way of life."
— MICHAEL HARRINGTON

THE JOY OF CENTS

"How apt the poor are to be proud."
—WILLIAM SHAKESPEARE, *TWELFTH NIGHT*

Poverty, as we all know, is the natural state of man, and *Suddenly Poor! A Guide for the Downwardly Mobile* is a guide for those proud, unshaken souls who are blissfully hitchiking along its freeways.

In this uncertain era of Reaganomics, when unsettling prime lending rates and the high cost of a humble cup of cappuccino are threatening to derail our customarily hopeful trains of thought about the future, it's nice to know there's something you can turn to when you've finally accepted that you're broke as hell and you're not gonna fake it anymore!

Our aim is to pass on to the Great Undrycleaned the timeless tenets of creative insolvency, acquainting those to the manner shorn with proper rules of pauperistic deportment, whether they concern gainful unemployment, coping with the bill collector, juggling social disengagements, keeping down appearances, or dressing for powerlessness.

Not to mention correct mental attitudes and a sense of discreet solidarity with the princely pauper throughout history. Only the most upright people have been poor! Whenever you find yourself trying to obscure, conceal, or otherwise behave sheepishly about your august diminishment, we encourage you to examine your conscience and ask, "Would Ralph Kramden have stood by quietly watching his building go co-op?" Or, "Would the resolutely abject Nazarene, unreachable in the desert for forty days and forty nights, have even *considered* springing for call-forwarding?"

Show a little pauper pride!

Who said that?

Match the Cheap Quip with the Quipster

George Bernard Shaw   Socrates   Jean Paul Getty

1. "If you know what you're worth, you're not worth enough."

2. "If you're going to save the world, you might as well do it at a profit."

3. "If you pick up a starving dog and make him prosperous, he will not bite you. This is the principal difference between a man and a dog."

Wimpy

H.L. Hunt

Mark Twain

4. "I think I have sufficient witness that I speak the truth, namely, my poverty."

5. "I will gladly pay you Tuesday for a hamburger today."

6. "If all economists were laid end to end, they would not reach a conclusion."

Answers: 1, Getty; 2, Hunt; 3, Twain; 4, Socrates; 5, Wimpy; 6, Shaw.

HOW DO YOU KNOW YOU'RE ONE OF THE NOUVEAU PAUVRE?

An informal checklist

Did you wake up this morning and grapple with the contorted shell of a toothpaste tube, cutting it open to scrape the last traces of its contents from its inner walls?

☐ Did you eat breakfast out of a week-old doggie bag you discovered was cowering behind the empty bacon package in the icebox?

☐ Did you wash it down with a cup of tepid water vaguely seasoned by a teabag pressed into service for the umpteenth time?

☐ Are safety pins rapidly becoming the main accessories in your wardrobe?

☐ Is the ring of the telephone as unpleasant as the ring around your collar?

☐ Did Gabby Hayes have more teeth than the comb in your back pocket?

☐ Do you find yourself collecting the deposit on last week's spent six-pack in order to get bus fare and purchase a newspaper, only to read that the government plans to spend $14 billion to explore the feasibility of constructing in the upper atmosphere a gigantic mirror that will be capable of scrutinizing the plaque on the teeth of every KGB agent west of Kamchatka?

☐ Finally, look at the the pen you're using to complete this checklist. Is it the same pen you've been using for your correspondence to your creditors? Have you and your spouse lately been gnawing at it with the same ferocious anxiety you normally reserve for filling out your tax forms? In other words, does the poor little Bic resemble your golden retriever's chew stick?

If the answer to even one of the above is a whimpered "yes," congratulations. You're one of the Nouveau Pauvre!

Squint into the mirror and face up to the truth: You're a Cash-Flow Cripple! A Strapped Soldier of Misfortune! A Parvenu of the Pinched! You can scarcely afford to pay attention, much less last month's bills! Forget the arms race; we're talking about the alms race!

It's time you learned to accept with alacrity the noble badge of financial flunkout, keeping your head high and your overhead low. How do you spell relief? We spell it P-A-U-P-E-R-D-O-M.

Paupers come in various sexes, ages, shapes, and sizes, but most particularly in various stages of duress, redress, and undress. Still, state-of-the-art pauperism isn't arrived at by accident. It requires careful fine-tuning and is born of practical percipience, trial-and-error strategies, and sagacious stick-to-itiveness. Just about everything, except, of course, self-denial.

The five stages of pauperism, unchanged since Job's storied setbacks in the biblical land of Uz, are:

1) Cash-Flow Problems
2) Slightly Pinched
3) Strapped
4) Flat Broke
5) Total Destitution

Does the very sight of this list quicken your pulse and fill your breast with a strange, ineffable stirring? If so, then you're probably already winding your way along the high road to the poorhouse.

There is much to be explained and understood about the five stages, their subtle evolution in history, and their edifying impact on the individual. So let's get started. Face it: you've probably got a lot of time to kill anyway.

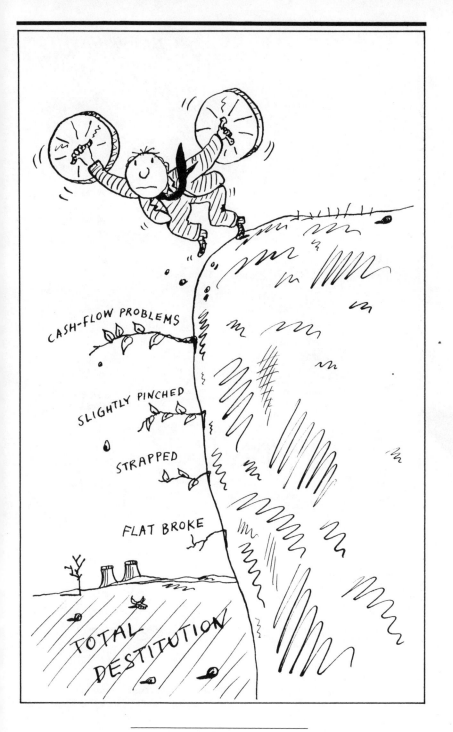

Day One of Pauperdom: Adam and Eve are evicted from Paradise.

A HISTORY OF THE POOR:
THE FORCED MARCH OF DIMES (or, ROME WASN'T BILKED IN A DAY)

There have always been those amongst us who have gracefully given themselves over, when need be, to the exquisite tranquility and peace of mind that lies at the other end of the rainbow, where billing cycles, debt consolidation, postdated checks, garnishments, ninety-day dunning letters, and property seizures pass into hazy memory.

The following timeline is a compelling recounting of the Pauper Chronicles. One glance at the epic saga—on a shoestring—and you'll understand why William Carlos Williams confessed, "It's the anarchy of poverty delights me."

Paleolithic Age
Cro-Magnon Have-Nots chalk IOUs on cave walls.

2620-2480 B.C.
Jews and other enslaved peoples build the Pyramids of Egypt's Fourth Dynasty—for free.

546 B.C.
Prince Siddhartha, better known as Buddha, renounces the luxury of his royal house. The monks that follow in his footsteps shun all worldly riches, using *The Wall Street Journal* solely for fishwrap.

120 A.D.
The era of indecent foreclosures: The unholy Roman Empire decrees that any debtor in default for more than ninety days can be sold into slavery or thrown to the lions.

1170
Wandering European troubadours (the Sammy Davis, Jr.'s of their day) spare no spiel in order to curry favor with the fat cats of the royal courts.

1298
Bare feet and sandals are no longer *de rigueur* among the friars; brocaded belts now gird their capon-stuffed stomachs.

400
St. Nicholas, a bishop in Asia Minor, wanders about in disguise, giving gifts to the needy.

1319
Craft guilds set aside "God's Penny," an occasional kitty that proves a humble windfall for the destitute.

1332
With dispensations and absolution going for top dollar, pure-of-heart paupers shudder, led to believe that they cannot afford the entrance fee to heaven.

1299
An iffy time for those who are out at the elbows, since they receive few handouts of gruel at the castle gate.

1348
The Black Plague appears. Typically, the poor do most of the dying.

1335
St. Martin, patron saint of the underprivileged, gives half his cloak to a wretch during a particularly frigid winter and thus inaugurates genuine trickle-down economics.

1372
French nobleman Amanieu d' Albret VI leaves one hundred livres for the dowries of "those poor young women whom I have deflowered, if they can be found."

1410
Monasteries, once austere cloisters dedicated to unstinting poverty and self-denial, become medieval equivalents of Club Med.

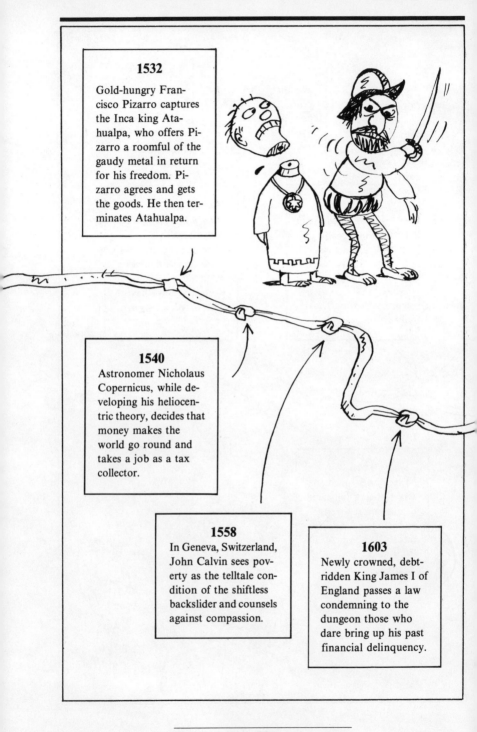

1532

Gold-hungry Francisco Pizarro captures the Inca king Atahualpa, who offers Pizarro a roomful of the gaudy metal in return for his freedom. Pizarro agrees and gets the goods. He then terminates Atahualpa.

1540

Astronomer Nicholaus Copernicus, while developing his heliocentric theory, decides that money makes the world go round and takes a job as a tax collector.

1558

In Geneva, Switzerland, John Calvin sees poverty as the telltale condition of the shiftless backslider and counsels against compassion.

1603

Newly crowned, debt-ridden King James I of England passes a law condemning to the dungeon those who dare bring up his past financial delinquency.

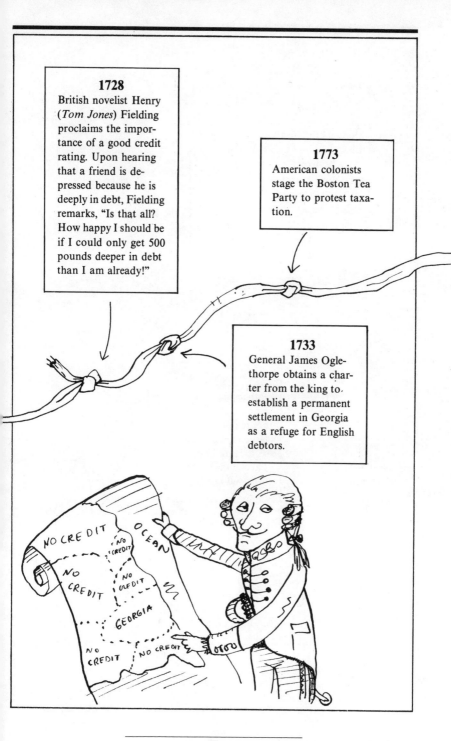

1728
British novelist Henry (*Tom Jones*) Fielding proclaims the importance of a good credit rating. Upon hearing that a friend is depressed because he is deeply in debt, Fielding remarks, "Is that all? How happy I should be if I could only get 500 pounds deeper in debt than I am already!"

1773
American colonists stage the Boston Tea Party to protest taxation.

1733
General James Oglethorpe obtains a charter from the king to establish a permanent settlement in Georgia as a refuge for English debtors.

1780
British literary genius Samuel Johnson is prudent enough to remark that "a decent provision for the poor is the true test of civilization."

1789
Marie Antoinette, wife of King Louis XVI, advocates junk food for the starving rabble.

1786
Publicly supported paupers in New Jersey are required to wear a large blue or red letter *P*, the forerunner of the Pauper Pride buttons in fashion today.

1790
The rabble, dubbed the *sans culottes* by the French ruling class, respond with a revolution.

1791
Wolfgang Amadeus Mozart composes a record-breaking 600 works for Europe's wealthiest archbishops and emperors. His services are bought for a song, however, and he dies in destitution at thirty-five.

1796
Sir William Arkwright patents a spinning machine. Sweatshops and child labor swiftly follow; workers are sometimes chained to their stations.

1826

Honest Abe Lincoln calls a log cabin his home, splits rails by day, and writes his lessons by firelight on the back of a shovel. Pauper ingenuity!

1816

Society for the Prevention of Pauperism is founded, while persecution of the penniless runs rampant in America.

April 10, 1849

Patent No.6281 is granted to Walter Hunt for the safety pin, which enables millions of paupers to keep their chins *and* trousers up.

1820

Female paupers in New England are awarded bedding by local officials to help attract industrious hubbies.

1848

Gold is discovered near John Sutter's prosperous sawmill in California. Sutter's workers' yen to get rich quick leaves Sutter flat busted.

1880

The Salvation Army makes its first American convert: "Ash-barrel Jimmy" Kemp, a noted Bowery boozehound, whose nickname stems from a tipsy tumble into the keg.

December 24, 1928

John D. Rockefeller, whose oil companies are earning a cool $400 million, gives each of the groundskeepers and maintenance workers at his splendid Pocantico estate a $5 Christmas bonus and the day off.

December 26, 1928

Returning to work the day after Christmas, the Pocantico staff discover that they have been docked $5 each for absenteeism.

1929

The Great Depression, or Halcyon Era of Hobohemia, begins. Paupers face the niggardliness of nature with sturdy savvy and sinewy flair. Seasoned veterans want to know what makes this depression so great, since the nation went through them in 1819, 1837, 1857, 1873, 1893, 1907, and 1921.

October, 1929

Variety records the stock market crash with the headline WALL STREET LAYS AN EGG.

December, 1929

Manhattan hotel clerks begin asking registrants, "You want a room for sleeping or jumping?"

March, 1933

FDR pledges a New Deal.

July 28-29, 1932

President Hoover permits General MacArthur to use tanks, tear gas, and bayonets to rout thousands of unemployed and poverty-stricken World War I veterans and their families from sprawling shantytowns in the nation's capital.

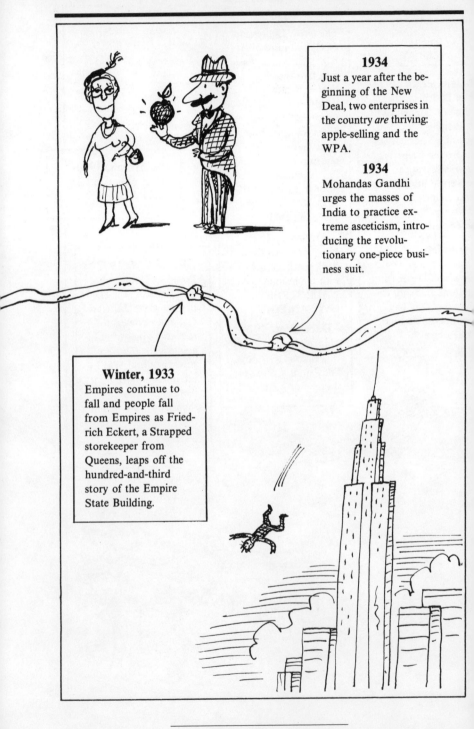

1934

Just a year after the beginning of the New Deal, two enterprises in the country *are* thriving: apple-selling and the WPA.

1934

Mohandas Gandhi urges the masses of India to practice extreme asceticism, introducing the revolutionary one-piece business suit.

Winter, 1933

Empires continue to fall and people fall from Empires as Friedrich Eckert, a Strapped storekeeper from Queens, leaps off the hundred-and-third story of the Empire State Building.

1972

Reporters discover that the New York Telephone Company receives a minimum of $70 million monthly in interest-free loans by wording its bills so that advance service charges appear to apply to the previous month. No one complains; the practice continues.

1973

Unwelcome panhandlers pressing the doorbell at the lavish Fort Lauderdale home of millionaire Ray Kroc, the McDonald's fast-food magnate, hear a familiar jingle, reminding them of the daily break they deserve but won't be getting at that residence.

1974

Jamaican reggae star Bob Marley unveils the Caribbean pauper's anthem, "Them Belly Full (But We Hungry)."

1977

During the critical U.S. gas and heating oil shortages, Treasury Secretary William Simon quips, "Many are cold but few are frozen."

1979
The Hunt brothers, billionaire speculators, burst the Silver Bubble after driving prices up so that thousands of Strapped grandmas can't get their tea services melted down fast enough.

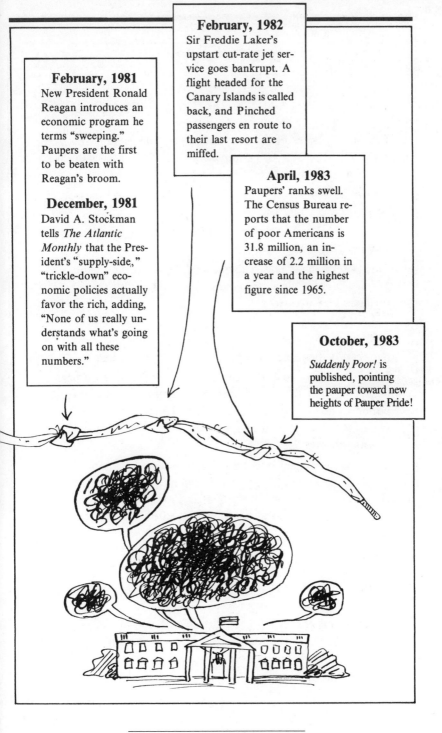

February, 1981
New President Ronald Reagan introduces an economic program he terms "sweeping." Paupers are the first to be beaten with Reagan's broom.

December, 1981
David A. Stockman tells *The Atlantic Monthly* that the President's "supply-side," "trickle-down" economic policies actually favor the rich, adding, "None of us really understands what's going on with all these numbers."

February, 1982
Sir Freddie Laker's upstart cut-rate jet service goes bankrupt. A flight headed for the Canary Islands is called back, and Pinched passengers en route to their last resort are miffed.

April, 1983
Paupers' ranks swell. The Census Bureau reports that the number of poor Americans is 31.8 million, an increase of 2.2 million in a year and the highest figure since 1965.

October, 1983
Suddenly Poor! is published, pointing the pauper toward new heights of Pauper Pride!

ADVERSARIES OF THE POOR

AN ENEMIES LIST

Croesus—Minter of the first gold coins, this wealth-obsessed king denied workman's compensation to the slaves who broke their backs mining Croesus' spare change.

Ayatollah Khomeini—First runner-up to his predecessor, the Shah, as a deluder of Iran's downtrodden.

Scrooge McDuck—Unkind to his web-footed friends, he cut Donald and Daisy out of his will.

Earl Blackwell—Created the annual "Best-Dressed" and "Worst-Dressed" lists, stealing the spotlight from those thrilled to be dressed at all.

Louis XIV—Landlord of Versailles, playground of rich twits and their toadies in the 1700s, he liked to sentence debt-prone paupers to the dungeon while luxuriating in his bed.

Mrs. Stuyvesant Fish ("Mame")—Turn-of-the-century hostess who once invited the Newport set to a sumptuous dinner honoring her pet chimpanzee. "Now the monkey and the swell must be accepted as interchangable types," the newspapers reported.

H. L. Hunt—The Texas oil billionaire served his luncheon guests drugstore sandwiches with typing paper for a napkin. He was drummed out of the Dallas Country Club for refusing to give to local charities. Asked to contribute to the restoration of a church at his birthplace, he sent five bucks.

Jean Paul Getty—The oil magnate disliked philanthropy intensely, kept a pay phone in his home, and would gladly wait for hours to bum a ride with an associate rather than spend money on a taxi.

Andreas and Jakob Fugger—Fourteenth century money-lenders who were the forerunners of the Rothschilds; their family name endures as one of history's great accidental misspellings.

Animal Gourmet—A doggie delicatessen on Manhattan's East Side; wealthy art collector and canine fancier Michele Bertolli once sampled the chicken supreme and exclaimed, "It was better than the chicken I had the other night at El Morocco!"

Miyamoto Musaschi—A seventeenth-century samurai who wrote a "guide for men who want to learn strategy," *The Book of Five Rings*. Japan's answer to the Harvard M.B.A., it counsels the cultivation of cold logic and cunning in business dealings. In pauper circles, the paperback edition of the book is best known for its thickness—exactly five-eights of an inch, ideal for inserting under the leg of a wobbly bar stool.

James Watt—Exterminator of the pauper's bottom-line freebies: fresh air, green grass, and shade trees.

Nancy Reagan—Most insensitive dinner belle since Marie Antoinette, she used a 1981 grant of $209,508 from the Knapp Foundation to buy a set of White House china.

Citibank—Customers with less than $5,000 on deposit are no longer considered worthy of teller service and must use the bank's cash machines, where computer screens are fond of flashing SORRY, I CAN'T DO THAT RIGHT NOW.

FRIENDS OF THE POOR

SOME MEMBERS OF THE MISFORTUNE 500

Job	Church mice
Rodney Dangerfield	Billy Carter
Emmett Kelly	Woody Guthrie
Henry David Thoreau	Vincent Van Gogh
Charlie Weaver	Hank Williams
Tom Waits	Fiorello La Guardia
F. W. Woolworth	Sinclair Lewis
Lao Tzu	Martin Luther King, Jr.
Minnie Pearl	Will Rogers
Saint Jude	W. E. B. Du Bois

CAN YOU SPOT THE CASH-FLOW CRIPPLE?

Answer: They're all tapped out! The man on the left was in securities, the chap in the middle was in marketing, and the guy on the right was in advertising. Now the trio are in hock up to their earlobes!

CASH-FLOW PROBLEMS

"I left my credit card in my other tux."

cash-flow problems (kash-flō präb-ləmz) *n, pl* Monetary questions, situations, or conditions of the once-comfortable upper middle class that can be alleviated only temporarily by making vague promises to caterers named Pierre in order to put off compensation of lawn doctors named Paul; i.e., to keep one's shirt when those around you are losing theirs and blaming it on you.

Here we see the average American family in the grip of a wave of classic arrears fears—garden-variety pocketbook panic. Employment of the heads of the household is currently in a state of abeyance, so motor-mouthed mutants calling themselves "credit counselors" have been writing and telephoning with unnerving regularity. And the coin of the realm that might put things in a more balanced position is missing in action, i.e., "The check is on the Concorde." It's a Cash-Flow Crisis. But is it?

First of all, since some amount of help is presumably on the way, it shouldn't be important *when it* arrives. Most creditors give you a grace period of one hundred days before they get huffy—and besides, it's common knowledge that the wealthy customarily pay their bills only once a year, no matter how large or small. If somebody gets *really* ruffled, tell them your cash assets may or may not be tied up in short-term convertible debentures—you have to consult your broker to be certain—and then take the kids camping (in the back yard) for six weeks.

But whatever you do, *don't* waste a millisecond worrying. Don't be what H. L. Mencken called the "booboisie." Hell, during the 1972 presidential campaign, Senator George McGovern's unpaid travel bills grew so large that his airline and car-rental cards were revoked. Did you see George walking point or dispatching AWAC planes to locate the postman? Of course not. Besides, everybody knows that bad debts are tax-deductible.

SOCIAL STUDIES IN THE 1980s:
KEEPING DOWN APPEARANCES

The Nouveau Pauvre often blend in with the passing parade. Thus, if you are on the lookout for kindred spirits, you must be attentive to subtleties. Consider this duo.

A securities analyst laid off seven months ago, she lives in a rent-controlled one-bedroom apartment just off the Loop in downtown Chicago. Gone is the 42-Gs-per-annum entanglement. With luck, she might keep Master-Card at bay for another half-year. The timeless lessons of this woman's trusty B.A. (from Sarah Lawrence; she "concentrated in" American social history, writing her thesis on "the hobo") have seeped back into her consciousness to lend her considerable perspective on her rapidly reductionist circumstances.

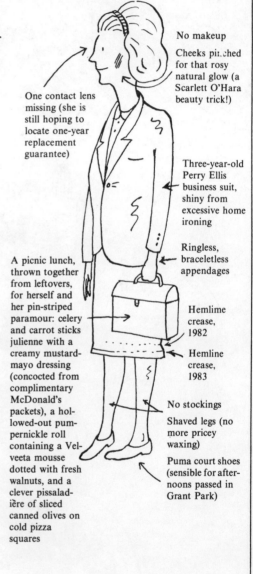

No makeup

Cheeks pinched for that rosy natural glow (a Scarlett O'Hara beauty trick!)

One contact lens missing (she is still hoping to locate one-year replacement guarantee)

Three-year-old Perry Ellis business suit, shiny from excessive home ironing

Ringless, braceletless appendages

A picnic lunch, thrown together from leftovers, for herself and her pin-striped paramour: celery and carrot sticks julienne with a creamy mustard-mayo dressing (concocted from complimentary McDonald's packets), a hollowed-out pumpernickle roll containing a Velveeta mousse dotted with fresh walnuts, and a clever pissaladière of sliced canned olives on cold pizza squares

Hemlime crease, 1982

Hemline crease, 1983

No stockings

Shaved legs (no more pricey waxing)

Puma court shoes (sensible for afternoons passed in Grant Park)

A slow-ripening candidate for the lower crust, this semi-trig onetime junior headhunter for an executive recruitment firm in Houston spent last April tacking in his hot-shot young ex-boss's rented thirty-foot skiff off the coast of Honolulu. He returned from vacation to confront the OPEC/North Sea oil glut and polite termination. Back home in the Windy City, he sometimes tends bar at the swank The 95th in the Hancock Building and rooms with a school chum (Lake Forest College).

Hair creeping over collar

Broad set of sagging shoulders from now abandoned workouts on Nautilus machine at former health club

Tight smile

$35 silk X'Andrini club tie

Vaguely spotted (damn those pigeons!) splurge from that last Hawaiian fling: one of those smart white cotton Christian Dior suits, nearly paid for

Stubborn stain from final ex-pense-account lunch (shrimps and clams Posilipo at Palm)

Squash bag containing portable library for long waits in the unemployment line: *Blue Highways, The End of the World News*

Scuffed low-vamp, braided-tassel loafers ($250 a pair); charged at Perkins Shearer in Denver while tracking a board-room mark

One dark blue sock, one dark brown sock— close enough

WORRIES

A   N   D

ANXIETIES

The worst that could possibly happen

1.

Bijan on Rodeo Drive might no longer take your
reservations to shop there.

2.

Your wife won't get the "Candy Bergen nose" and
"Susan Sarandon chin" plastic surgery you promised
her as an anniversary present.

3.

You'll lose your prime table across from Philip
Johnson at The Four Seasons.

4.

You'll have to forfeit your mooring
at the Boca Raton Yacht Club.

5.

The IRS will send you to jail for tax evasion and there
won't be any openings at the "right" country-club
lockups, like Allenwood Minimum Security
Prison in Pennsylvania.

UNNECESSARY

Okay, so the better bill collectors are finding their mark and taking their toll. While you're giving them their due, are you holding out on yourself? Have you stopped for a minute to assess all the liquid assets that are sublimely unessential to your existence? All the cluttersome possessions and expensive practices that you could, to your good fortune and, er, credit, eliminate? Make a complete inventory of every blessed thing in your house of any value and begin thinking of these objects in terms of public auctions, yard and rummage sales, and pawnshops.

Then there's the all-important category of returnable merchandise, often heralded by a card or a sticker that reads: "Money-Back Guarantee If Not Completely Satisfied!" Are you *sure* you're *Completely Satisfied* with that Porsche 911SC Cabriolet you treated yourself to just before the senior vice-president took you out for the surprise farewell lunch? Doesn't the car seem to lack torque on those tight curves? And how about that faint whirring noise when you're downshifting? Or consider the microwave oven in which you've cooked the last three Thanksgiving turkeys: the dark meat has always turned out a tad dry, hasn't it? Check out the Sony Walkman you bought last fall; it's sounding a little tinny on the highs and rumbly on the lows, and the right headphone is a little dimmer than the left, right?

Right! So get what you deserve—a refund! By all means, don't be afraid of letting go. Since biblical times, people have been coping creatively with impending liquidity crises. Had Noah followed our advice, he would have weathered his own storm in style. As it was, he wound up stuck on a mountaintop with two of everything! Who needs that kind of headache?!

N E C E S S I T I E S

Here are some things you can *definitely* afford to surrender:

RECREATION
Ski trip to St. Moritz
21-day tour of the Orient
Opening night gala at the Met
Health-club membership
Cottage in Crete

HOUSEWARES
Cuisinart
Simac Pastamatic machine
Il Gelatano ice-cream maker
Waterford crystal (especially the Dunmore biscuit barrel)
Gailstyn copper fondue set and chafing dish
Le Creuset cookware
Wusthof-Trident cutlery
Reed & Barton 18th-century sterling dinnerware
Maxim espresso-cappuccino machine

HOME CONVENIENCES/TOYS
Soloflex machine
NordicTrack cardiovascular cross-country skiing motion exercizer
Sanyo Beta Scan VCR
Brother Correctronic typewriter
Canon checkbook calculator
Minolta XG-1 35mm camera
Kloss Novabeam Model Two video projector
Bang & Olufsen Beocenter 7700-S combination turntable, tuner, and tape deck

IBM 67K home computer
Donkey Kong and Ms. Pac-Man home video games
Amana microwave oven
Deluxe Bonaire 1000 air cleaner-ionizer
Panabrator II massage wand
Portable Jacuzzi whirlpool
Davwar bidet

HOME FURNISHINGS
Charles P. Rogers solid brass bed
Levolor designer blinds
Eames chairs
Dakota Jackson desk set
Yamaha baby grand piano
All original paintings, prints, lithographs, sculpture, and objets d'art

JEWELRY, CLOTHES, AND SUNDRIES
Concord Mariner SG watch
Van Cleef & Arpels pearl earrings
Princess Marcella Borghese Lumina Colour Cache
Castleberry knits
Jeffrey Banks blazer
Niki De Saint Phalle Eau de Toilette (in First Edition sculpture flacon)
Susan Bennis-Warren Edwards shoes
Dimitri couture suits
Tiffany quartz watches
Jhane Barnes slacks
Elancyl massage kit
Ralph Lauren Lisette Claire dresses
Liberty of London jumpsuits

Saint Laurent Rive Gauche
separates
Giorgio Armani tops
Pierre Cardin cologne
Anne Klein snakeskin belt and
handbag
Adam Beall gabardine
Charles Jourdan pumps

TRANSPORTATION
Air travel. (It's always made you
jumpy anyhow.)
• In the process, resign from all
those members-only preflight
lounges. And while you're at it,
why not lose the Kaypro II
double-disk-drive portable
computer you used on those first-
class flights? There's barely elbow
room on Amtrak to begin with.

COMMUNICATIONS
Phone beeper.
• Nobody but a physician should
own one in the first place, and a
lot of people still mistake them
for pacemakers. Besides, consid-
ering the kinds of calls you'll be
getting from now on, you're
better off if you're tough to reach.

SUBSCRIPTIONS
(mail-order catalogues)
Horchow
Orvis
Intimique
Moat House
Albert S. Smyth Company, Inc.
Spiegel
Gump's
Brownstone Studio
Draper's of Southern California
Chatham Fields, Inc.
Boston Proper
Britex

Jos. A. Bank Clothiers
Brooks Brothers
Walpole's
Saks Fifth Avenue

CLUBS
Myopia Hunt Club

CARDS
American Express Gold Card
Carte Blanche
Neiman Marcus
Diners Club
Bonwit-Teller

SHOPPING
Boutiques, specialty shops, gourmet delicatessens
• Focus on discount designer
outlets and antique clothing
haunts. Have you seen the fall
fashions? Japanese pajamas and
clam-diggers, thin-lapel drip-dry
suits and frayed, soiled-looking
drab rags that Bloomingdale's is
calling "Street Couture." The
Eisenhower Era is back; the
fashion emphasis is on "sensible
wear" and the conservatism of the
1950s. You've got all that stuff in
mothballs or in boxes in the
garage! As for groceries, everybody knows that Pathmark,
Piggly Wiggly, Ralph's, and Sav-
On Drugs are now chic.

ENTERTAINING
Restaurants.
• Fancy, middling, or otherwise,
you have no business in such
places. Make up a few sirloin
meat loaves, throw a paper-plate
party in your basement, and call
it a Bomb Shelter Blow-Out. Get
hip!

CASH-FLOW
D I A L O G U E

"Hello, Mr. Deddbeate?"

"Yes?"

WHAT HE SAYS: *"This is Mr. Gouger. Did you get my bill?"*
(**WHAT HE MEANS:** *"I've been trying for some time to get you on the horn, and I'm a little concerned."*)

WHAT HE SAYS: *"Nice to hear from you! Long time no see! I've got a bill here, somewhere, I guess. Is it yours?"*
(**WHAT HE MEANS:** *"Damn it! How could I have been so dopey as to answer the phone myself?"*)

WHAT HE SAYS: *"Oh well, I just sent you a bill, and you should have received it by now."*

(**WHAT HE MEANS:** *"I've got a funny feeling you're going to try and welch on me."*)

WHAT HE SAYS: *"Hold on, let me see if I can find it."*

(**WHAT HE MEANS:** *"You think you've got me where you want me, eh?"*)

WHAT HE SAYS: *"No problem, I just need to know if we can collect."*

(**WHAT HE MEANS:** *"Don't play dumb with me. Your kids have been screening your phone calls for the last month, and yesterday you put your dog on and had him bark into the receiver."*)

WHAT HE SAYS: *"Hmmm, can't seem to locate the letter. I'm sure it's around, but my accountant's on vacation in Belize."*

(**WHAT HE MEANS:** *"Obviously, I put the bill on the bottom of my birdcage, with the rest of the notices you send me."*)

WHAT HE SAYS: *"I quite understand. But I can expect payment within the month?"*

(**WHAT HE MEANS:** *"Aha! Just as I thought. If I don't get tough with you fella, I'll see my money the day that there's ice-boating in Hell!"*)

WHAT HE SAYS: *"Absolutely!"*

(WHAT HE MEANS: *"NEXT MONTH?! You must be a standup comedian! I have three dollars in my checking account!!")*

WHAT HE SAYS: *"You realize, of course, that payment is long overdue."*

(WHAT HE MEANS: *"I wouldn't trust you with a ball of lint. Once my lawyers step in, you won't know what building fell on you.")*

WHAT HE SAYS: *"Yes, and I understand your concern."*

(WHAT HE MEANS: *"Don't bully me, Bozo.")*

WHAT HE SAYS: *"Very well, I look forward to receiving your check immediately."*

(WHAT HE MEANS: *"I've got a cousin in Newark, New Jersey, who'd gladly ram his Lincoln Continental straight into your kneecaps.")*

WHAT HE SAYS: *"No problem! Have a good day!"*

(WHAT HE MEANS: *"What a bloodsucker! Well, the next time you call this number, this house will probably be a vacant lot, and I'll be living in a lean-to in the Yucatan. Buzz off!")*

A CASH-FLOW NO-NO

If you're allegedly having some difficulty meeting your operating expenses, it's unwise to allegedly meet in a Los Angeles hotel room with possible undercover government agents who are allegedly willing to sell you more than fifty-nine pounds of uncut cocaine with an alleged street value of approximately $6.5 million.

SLIGHTLY PINCHED

"Buddy, can you spare a twenty?"

slightly pinched (slīt́-ly pĭncht) *adj* Strained financial condition in which offhand remarks from friends like "Give yourself some credit!" take on a special poignancy.

Here's where real creative reasoning first begins to set in. Remember, impending poverty is the stepmother of genius. After you've auctioned off the Atari and the Vera sheets and all the rest of the blatant expendables, you come to realize that your closets and living spaces used to be horribly glutted with shiny hardware that did little to enhance the quality of your life. All that costly junk did do was separate you from your essential ingenuity, your exquisite, innate knack for reinventing yourself and your environment to mutual advantage. Now that the warehouse is a home again, you have room to move—around in it, that is. And with a mind less burdened by the specter of burglary!

UNNECESSARY NECESSITIES

Happily, the dead weight still in inventory is a damn sight easier to spot!

TRANSPORTATION

Automobile

• Mercedes, Subaru, Rambler American—makes no difference. That hulking metal moneyeater squatting in your driveway, leaking oil, collecting grime and rust, trapping all your loose change under the seats, has got to go. Wash the big dumb doorstop one last time and get a few dozen tirekickers over to haggle about it. Then pocket the highest bid and start riding the bus with *your* kind of people!

COMMUNICATIONS

Call-forwarding, call-waiting, answering service, phone machine

CLUBS

Junior League

CARDS

MasterCard, Visa, gas and car-rental plastic

SHOPPING

Supermarkets (stick to farmer's markets and roadside stands)

RECREATION

Cable television

Theater (except for an occasional half-price ticket)

Concerts (except for open-air affairs when the sound systems are good enough to carry the sound beyond the paying seats)

Ballet

Fishing trips

Beauty parlors

Golf

Day of downhill skiing at Loon Mountain

Gravity guiding inversion boots

Family trip to Chinatown

HOME CONVENIENCES

Dishwasher

Freezer

Toaster oven

Waffle iron

Ginsu cooking knife

Blender

Electric can-opener

Electric coffee-grinder

Automatic drip coffee-maker

Electric mixer

Silver tea service (should have gone last time, but it was a family heirloom)

JEWELRY, CLOTHES, AND SUNDRIES

Seiko watch

Gloria Vanderbilt jeans

Ralph Lauren polo shirts

anything Gucci (including auto key chains)

Jogging clothes

Tennis outfits

UNNECESSARY

Roots espadrilles
Your patent-leather
    dancing pumps
American Tourister luggage
Blassport sportswear
Jantzen/Sperry-Sider sailing
    wear (you gave up the yacht-club
    membership a while ago)
All athletic equipment, from
    AMF Head tennis rackets to the
    badminton set

SUBSCRIPTIONS
Money
Architectural Digest
Esquire
The New Yorker
House & Garden
Fortune
New York
California
Glamour
Cosmopolitan
Vogue
Guns & Ammo
Vanity Fair
Consumer Reports
The Atlantic
Travel & Leisure
Sailing
Savvy
On Cable
Wall Street Journal
New York Review of Books
Time
Geo

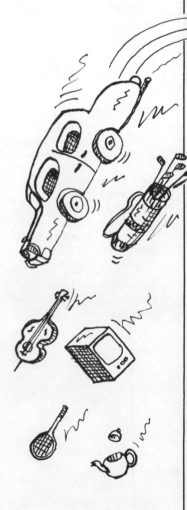

NECESSITIES

HOME FURNISHINGS
● Minimalist home decorating is the rage! Get rid of all unessential furniture: coffee tables, side tables, pool tables, dining-room tables, dressing table (keep the kitchen table and a card table), rocking chairs, footstools, Laz-E-Boy, all mirrors but one, hat racks, lawn and patio furniture.

PINCHED PASTIMES

Television shows, books, and movies to enhance your mood

TELEVISION

Beverly Hillbillies
The Flintstones
The Honeymooners
The Real McCoys
The Waltons
Top Cat
How to Marry a Millionaire
Sanford and Son
Upstairs, Downstairs
Wagon Train
You Bet Your Life
Break the Bank
(I Remember) Mama
Hee Haw
The Good Life
The Abbott and Costello Show
The Millionaire
The Goldbergs
Good Times
Green Acres
Lassie

No place like home: the Kramdens and the Nortons were cheap dates.

BOOKS

The Human Comedy
by William Saroyan

Have You Seen Their Faces
by Margaret Bourke-White

As I Lay Dying
by William Faulkner

Cannery Row
by John Steinbeck

Errol Flynn demonstrates the Sherwood Forest equivalent of
MasterCard in THE ADVENTURES OF ROBIN HOOD (1938).

Hard Times
by Studs Terkel

A Distant Mirror
by Barbara Tuchman

Paper Money
by Adam Smith

Studs Lonigan
by James T. Farrell

Tarzan
by Edgar Rice Burroughs

*When Bad Things Happen
to Good People*
by Harold Kushner

Leaves of Grass
by Walt Whitman

Roughing It
by Mark Twain

The Call of the Wild
by Jack London

You Can't Go Home Again
by Thomas Wolfe

MOVIES

It's A Wonderful Life
(1946), starring James
Stewart & Donna Reed

My Man Godfrey (1936),
starring Carole Lombard
& William Powell

*Mister Deeds Goes to
Town* (1936), starring Gary
Cooper

Little Women (1933),
starring Joan Bennett

Pocketful of Miracles (1961), starring Bette Davis

Oliver! (1968)

Great Expectations (1946), starring John Mills & Alec Guinness

A Christmas Carol (1938), starring Reginald Owen

The Grapes of Wrath (1940), starring Henry Fonda

My Fair Lady (1964), starring Rex Harrison & Audrey Hepburn

The Adventures of Robin Hood (1938), starring Errol Flynn

Mary Poppins (1964), starring Julie Andrews & Dick Van Dyke

Sounder (1972), starring Cicely Tyson & Paul Winfield

Being There (1979), starring Peter Sellers

Gold Diggers of 1937, starring Dick Powell & Joan Blondell

On the Waterfront (1954), starring Marlon Brando

Paper Moon (1973), starring Ryan & Tatum O'Neal

Salt of the Earth (1954), starring Will Geer

Hard Times (1975), starring Charles Bronson

Apple Annie, street vendor, on a minimalist coffee break in Bette Davis's POCKETFUL OF MIRACLES (1961).

1040

THE TAX RETURN OF YOUR DREAMS
Federal Income Tax Form

1984

Your first name and initial (if joint return, also give spouse's name and initial—unless you don't feel like it)

Last name (or current alias)

Your Social Security number (round off to the nearest hundred)

Present home address (or an untraceable mail drop)

PRESIDENTIAL ELECTION CAMPAIGN	Do you want $1 from each candidate's fund before they have a chance to fritter the money away on bumper stickers and Styrofoam boaters?　Yes ___ No	*Note:* Checking "Yes" will not increase your tax or reduce your refund

FILING STATUS (Check any box you please)

1 ☐ Single
2 ☐ Married
3 ☐ Eager to be either

4 ☐ Undecided
5 ☐ Coy about it

6 ☐ Head of household
7 ☐ Freeloading joker
8 ☐ Deeply private person

EXEMPTIONS
(Always check the box labeled *yourself* or *somebody else*. Check other boxes as the mood stirs you.)

9a ☐ Yourself or somebody else
b ☐ Spouse
c ☐ Chippie
d ☐ Roué
e ☐ One-night stand

f ☐ 65 or under
g ☐ 65 or over
h ☐ Under suspicion of being in over your head

i ☐ Blind
j ☐ Soft contacts
k ☐ Easily distracted

Other dependents (up to three nonaquatic pets allowed)

Names _____ Relationship _____ Number of months lived in or near your home _____

Number of exemptions (a working subtotal) _____

INCOME
(Check Yes or No box)

10 Do you wish to conceal your income?　☐ Yes　☐ No
11 Have you seen *Gandhi?*　☐ Yes　☐ No
12 Would you like a special *Gandhi* deduction? Say, $1,000?　☐ Yes　☐ No

			Yes	No
15	Would you like a new you?		☐ Yes	☐ No
16	Could you use some rent money, royalties, profitable partnerships, estates, trusts?			
17	Did you see the episode of *The Honeymooners* where Ralph thought the IRS was going to audit him?		☐ Yes	☐ No
18	It was pretty funny, eh?		☐ Yes	☐ No
19	Do you think the Eisenhower dollar showed Ike's good side?		☐ Yes	☐ No
20	Would you like someone to rough up your mother-in-law?		☐ Yes	☐ No
21	Just give her a good scare?		☐ Yes	☐ No
22	Should we dry up and blow away?		☐ Yes	☐ No
23	Total income (unless the query annoys you) ___		☐ Yes	☐ No

TAX COMPUTATION

24	Subtract your age from your IQ for adjusted gross income	24 ___
25	Divide your license-plate number by your waist size and then double it twice for another fat check from out of the blue	25 ___
26	Multiply the insults you endured from your former employer by the sick days you never took and then book a flight to the South of France—we'll meet you at the gate with the cash total	26 ___

CREDITS

27	Credit for the elderly	27 ___
28	Credit for the cross-eyed	28 ___
29	Credit for the gap-toothed	29 ___
30	Extra credit	30 *wow*

REFUND

31	If line 23 is four times line 25, enter amount desired	31 ___
32	If line 31 doesn't satisfy you, multiply it by your dental bills	32 ___
33	If line 24 isn't low enough, consider a lobotomy	33 ___

PLEASE SIGN HERE

Under penalty of usury, we agree to give this return only the most cursory examination, and process all monies due to you with all deliberate speed. Could we have your autograph?

Signature _____ Date _____

STRA

PPED!

strapped (străpt) *adj* Dire no-dough malady characterized by slight shortness of breath and of trousers.

WHEN THE WHEREABOUTS OF YOUR WALLET IS NO MORE IMPORTANT THAN THE WHEREABOUTS OF YOUR CUFFLINKS, AND YOU BEGIN TO RESEMBLE THE PHOTO ON YOUR DRIVER'S LICENSE.

THE GREAT CHANGE SEARCH:

BURIED TREASURE IN A BUSTED HOUSEHOLD

Guess where the money's at!

Answers:

- In desk and bureau drawers: foreign currency left over from business trips and vacations in Bermuda
- In child's coin collection displayed in frame on wall
- In penny loafers; inside all other shoes in closets
- In side compartments of totebags and suitcases
- In coat, pants, sweater, and dress pockets
- Under the rugs
- In old pocketbooks
- Under cushions of couch and easy chairs
- In cuffs of pants in closet
- Behind and under refrigerator, stove, cabinets, and in utility drawers
- In piggybanks, penny collections in juice jars
- Also, assemble all grocery coupons, and don't forget about returnable bottles and cans!

MORE UNNECESSARY NECESSITIES

HOUSEWARES
The daily china

TRANSPORTATION
Bus and subway

COMMUNICATIONS
Long-distance calls

CLUBS
Rotary Club

CARDS
Twenty-four-hour banking card

SHOPPING
Purchases, period.

RECREATION
Movies
Plays (unless high school or
   college productions)
Television
Old phonograph records

**JEWELRY, CLOTHES,
AND SUNDRIES**
Grandma's mink
Your graduation ring
Earrings
Cufflinks
Your children's Sunday School
   attendance pins
Running shoes
Your wedding tux

Sights for Poor Eyes
(On a Clear Day You Can See Foreclosure)

1. Opera glasses   2. Tinted contacts   3. Foster Grants   4. Groucho glasses   5. Shaded eyes

Which bespectacled individual is Strapped?

Answer: No. 4. No. 3 is Greta Garbo—you don't have to be Strapped to want to be left alone.

The Last Supper:

Poormel's Menu *

LEFTOVER LEFTOVERS:
A CUPBOARD-CLEANING FEAST

Hors d'oeuvres
Carrot & Potato Peel Melée
Burner-Toasted Bread Crusts
Salted Corn Flakes

Soup
Ketchup & Water Bisque

Beverages
Sparking Tap Water
Tang, 1981

Entrees
Hamburger Helper (vegetarian style)
Spam à la Karo Syrup

Vegetable
Popcorn

Desserts
Ritz Cracker Mock Apple Pie
Kid's Halloween Candy, October 1982

———

*Dinner napkins courtesy White Cloud; glassware courtesy Smuckers jams,
Holiday Inn, Sau-Sea shrimp cocktail, and Dixie; lighting courtesy Con-Ed
billing dept.; table service available at all finer 7-Elevens*

With apologies to Gourmet *magazine.*

STRAPPED
CLASSICS

A gallery of the gallant few in film lore who have been truly inspiring to the newly perspiring debtor.

THE COAL MINER'S DAUGHTER (1980): Sissy Spacek smokes on Tobacco Road as Loretta Lynn.

A CHRISTMAS CAROL (1938): Reginald Owen is a sweet-and-sour Scrooge.

GONE WITH THE WIND (1939):
Vivien Leigh's cents-less Scarlett O'Hara
is street-smart.

WHAT COLOR IS YOUR BUMBERSHOOT?

NEW YORK (Zodiac News Service 10/27/75)—A beggar can earn about $17,000 a year simply by panhandling, according to a survey conducted by a newspaper here. The *New York Post* assigned one of its reporters to ask for spare change during a single eight-hour day. Despite New York's highly publicized financial woes, the reporter, Gene Weingarten, collected $48.96. At that rate, a panhandler would take home $12,729 a year—equivalent to a gross salary of $17,100.

FLAT BROKE

Life in the Fasting Lane

flat broke (flăt brōk) *adj* Having no more chance of acquiring pocket change than of acquiring a change of pockets.

Consider the married couple in the diagram. How can you be certain they're Poor? Well, the dead giveaway is the calm, focused look in their eyes. Gone is the furrowed brow of the Slightly Pinched era, or the blank or distant gaze of the Strapped stage. These people are feeling good about themselves for the first time in months. With no unemployment compensation remaining, they've begun to reach beyond themselves, to look back at shiny objects on the sidewalks. He's proud of how well his Papa Hemingway beard is shaping up, and with her tousled hair and the smart outfit she's made out of her old silk drapes, she reminds herself of Lee Remick in *Baby, The Rain Must Fall.*

She's gone vegetarian, with the emphasis on nuts and berries, but his slight paunch is a sign of the Midtown Manhattan Diet:

- breakfast—two glazed chocolate Dunkin' Donuts; black coffee with three sugars
- lunch—a slice of Sicilian pizza with extra cheese; one Hostess apple pie; coffee with three sugars
- dinner—six-pack of Schmidt's beer; three potato knishes; a brownie
- midnight snack—three stiff shots of Old Forrester; one pint can of Foster's lager (chaser)

Still, both stay in shape with such daily aerobics as frantic penny searches, cockroach chases, and brisk walks to and from the local bookstore, where they read the *New York Times* bestseller list in installments.

DRESSING <u>FOR</u> POWERLESSNESS

The windblown look, tied back with shoelace; split ends snipped by friends

Cut using a baseball cap with brim torn off as a guide

Brut splash cologne cut with tap water preserves a veneer of lapsed urbanity

Brushed with baking soda

Sagging bulge on left side of shapeless jacket, signaling that inside breast pocket is the last good one

Brooks Brothers, the Oxford collar badly frayed (and it's been reversed); a back-drawer holdover from college days. Monogramed initials on pocket and cuff are those of old schoolmate

Breezily braless

Mismatched buttons, home-sewn with different colors of thread

From another, similar suit of older vintage; cuffs have been folded down and pressed out

Chipped leather, pulled back to the last new notch (made with a fork)

No socks

Keds tennis sneakers with holes in toes (pauper classic)

Last half-serviceable set of Florsheim wing-tips, curling up at the toes; burgeoning holes in soles are covered up with squares of cardboard cut from record-album jackets (Linda Ronstadt's lips visible in left shoe)

WHAT'S YOUR BAG?

Which piece of luggage best complements your Flat-Broke status?

1. Louis Vuitton satchel

2. Straw tote, left over
from 1976 Bahamas trip

3. Battered Halliburton
briefcase

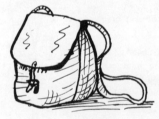

4. Canvas L. L.
Bean camp bag

5. Brown paper
sack, 5-pound test

Answer: L.L. Bean bag for the rough-and-ready pauper who no longer
spends weekends boating off Marina del Rey.

Things Anyone in Your Position Should Be Prepared to

GIVE UP

HOUSEWARES
Housewares

HOME CONVENIENCES
Electricity

TRANSPORTATION
Bicycles

COMMUNICATIONS
Home phone

CARDS
Business cards

CLUBS
Weight-Watchers

SUBSCRIPTIONS
"Occupant" mail (you're about to be evicted)

SHOPPING
Swap meets

RECREATION
Pets

THE FLAT BROKE
HALL OF FAME

Ratso Rizzo (Dustin Hoffman) planning his day
in **MIDNIGHT COWBOY** (1969).

The Little Tramp (Charlie Chaplin) is lord
of the manner in his curbside villa.

Tom Joad (Henry Fonda) helping his mother plan a
permanent vacation in **THE GRAPES OF WRATH** (1940).

Playtime in a pauper health spa
in **IT'S A WONDERFUL LIFE** (1946) starring Jimmy Stewart.

The carefree **Bowery Boys** share an
afternoon nap in their backstreet chateau.

THE PENNY SEARCH

(or, Harnessing the Law of Cent-Trifugal Force)

Where to look:

1. Between the cracks in the floorboards
2. Behind the moldings
3. In the linings of the clothes piled on the couch which are en route to the thrift shop
4. On the windowsills
5. Behind the radiators
6. Under the linoleum

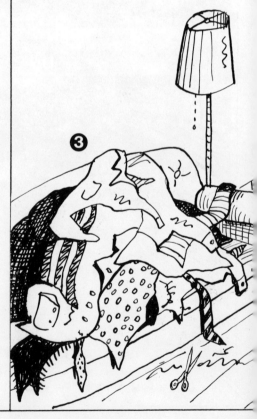

③

Posturepedic

SOD

Choose from seasonally soft to fairweather firm turf— A healthful, richly fragrant alternative to the conventional mattress: Stretched out like a log, you'll sleep just like a lamb!

HAYFIELD FUTON: A form-fitting bedding of sweetly tranquilizing resilience, perfect for the impromptu nap.

HI-RISER MEADOW MOSS: The open sky's the limit with this hillside sleeper, for those who like their shut-eye on a Posturemagic angle on the north side of a sheltering oak

KENTUCKY BLUE BOXSPRING: Unusually crisp support in a year-round sward—that's what you'll like about the South!

CRABGRASS LAWN COT: You'll nod out with the ease of a nanny-goat on this sturdy surface; ideal for those with back complaints.

18TH HOLE PASTURE PALLET: A bouncy bunk that fits your tired bones to a "tee." Cuddlesome comfort like you never got in the cradle!

STAGE FIVE

TOTAL DESTITUTION

"You Have Absolutely Nothing Left to Lose!"

Total Destitution (tō-tăl des-tə-t(y)ü-shən) *n* Peace of mind without a piece of the action.

Bet you never thought you'd make it this far, right? And at such an exhilarating pace! Well, you can pack up your troubles in your old kit bag and grin from ear to ear because you literally don't have a care in the world. It's a hobo jungle out there, and you've got the run of the place as you embark upon a life unfettered by billing cycles and debt-consolidation loans. Your social calendar is free and clear, and on your birthday your friends, family, and loved ones have the luxury of deciding what to give the person who has nothing.

In this unburdened stage you've got both feet on the ground (to put it bluntly) and *anything* is a luxury. Clothes fit better, food is more appetizing, your time is your own, and you've even begun to appreciate the way your mother-in-law decorates her apartment. Whether stalking the wild asparagus or doing some light reading in a classy hotel lobby, you've got the world on a shoestring. So pick yourself up, dust yourself off, and start all over again!

THE BEST & THE SLIGHTEST:
THE LAST THINGS YOU'LL EVER NEED!

Soap & toiletries
A fixed address
A line of work
A personal agenda
A sense of responsibility

LEAVING WHAT'S LEFT BEHIND

TRANSPORTATION
Shoes

COMMUNICATIONS
Pay phones

CLUBS
Club soda

CARDS
Postcards

SHOPPING
Window shopping

Good Benchkeeping

PROPER MAINTENANCE
OF YOUR MUNICIPAL
PIED-À-TERRE

IF PRODUCT OR PERFORMANCE DEFECTIVE
Good Benchkeeping
GUARANTEES
REPLACEMENT OR REFUND TO CONSUMER

YOUR OWN SQUIRREL-ROAST RECIPE!
BAKE SOME CRABAPPLE COBBLER!
HOW TO MAKE DANDELION WINE!

BOHEMIAN RHAPSODIES

Melodies to whistle while you daydream:

- "I Got Plenty o' Nuttin'"
- "Don't Fence Me In"
- "I Sold My Heart to the Junkman"
- "Easy Come, Easy Go"
- "We're in the Money"
- "In a Shanty in Old Shanty Town"
- "There'll Be Some Changes Made"
- "Easy Street"
- "I've Got the Sun in the Morning and the Moon at Night"
- "I Don't Know Where I'm Going But I'm on My Way"
- "Oh! How I Hate to Get Up in the Morning"
- "Pennies From Heaven"
- "Sing for Your Supper"
- "Look for the Silver Lining"
- "Yes! We Have No Bananas"
- "The Best Things in Life Are Free"
- "Show Me the Way to Go Home"
- "I'm Just a Vagabond Lover"
- "Singin' in the Rain"
- "Got the Bench, Got the Park, But I Haven't Got You"
- "I Found a Million-Dollar Baby in a Five and Ten Cent Store"
- "Tomorrow"

LAST RESORTS: PERMANENT VACATIONS ON THE OLD BUM NETWORK

A ROW BOAT TO CHINA

A STROLL AROUND THE EQUATOR

DOGGIE PADDLE TO PANGO-PANGO

Boxcar TO PATAGONIA

HITCHHIKING UP THE HIMALAYAS

Five Fabulous Getaways You Don't Have to Return From!

THE PEN IS MIGHTIER THAN THE HOARD!

There is one pleasant opportunity for financial reversal that we've put off mentioning until you absolutely, definitely have the free time and the unfettered mind to work on it—a book. After all, in a democracy, there are few woes that can't be transmuted into hard cash through the miracle of hard- and softbound personal sagas. So sit down and record your sense of loss, not forgetting to include lots of dramatic anecdotes. If you are also fortunate enough to have had abusive and/or psychotic parents, a prominent unfaithful spouse, or an affair with a high-ranking public official, you'd better nail down an agent as soon as you complete a first draft.

Some suggested titles:

- *Chronicle of a Debt Foretold*
- *Rags Time*
- *The Thorn Bushes*
- *The Whole Dearth Catalogue*
- *Slim Prospects in Thirty Days*
- *The Book of Shit Lists*
- *Real Bums Don't Eat Much*
- *Jane Fonda's Out-of-Workbook*

But whatever you scribble, don't write off the film, television, and merchandising rights. That's where the real lucre is!

THE ROAD UP:
THE SUM ALSO RISES

Enjoy your fling while you can, because before you know it
you'll be back at the grind. The economy is doomed to re-
cover; the Bureau of Labor Statistics predicts that some 24
million jobs will be available between 1978 and 1990. As it is,
people are always trying to pull one another out of the gutter
when they're just getting comfortable. Witness Eliza Doolittle
and her accursed voice coach! Soon you'll be taking the
Cuisinart out of hock, Fido out of the pound, and your coffee
black from the breakfast cart outside the boardroom. There'll
be reports to write, flow charts to analyze, planes to catch,
and no time for any more adventures at the other end of the
rainbow. This time next year, the smiling Joe in the crumpled
fedora who once shared his mulligan stew so freely may be
auditing you!

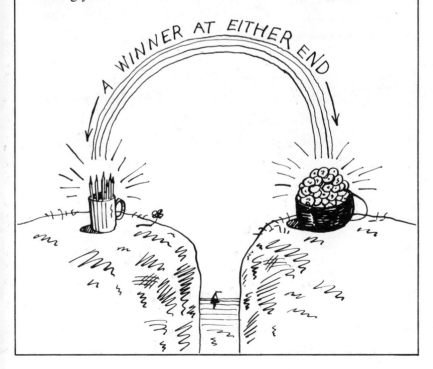

> **"I** don't want to see poverty abolished.
> Too much good has come of it."
>
> —ROBERT FROST

CREDITS & ACKNOWLEDGEMENTS

Page 1: "The Hardship of Accounting". From THE POETRY OF ROBERT FROST edited by Edward Connery Lathem. Copyright © 1936 by Robert Frost. Copyright © 1969 by Holt, Rinehart and Winston. Reprinted by permission of Holt, Rinehart and Winston, Publishers.

Page 72: Hand lettering by Ina Saltz

PHOTOGRAPHS

Pages 16, 49, 73 and 91: © Don Hamerman

Page 53: Wide World Photos

Page 60: From "The Honeymooners". Courtesy of Peekskill Enterprises, Inc.

Page 61: From the United Artists release "ADVENTURES OF ROBIN HOOD" © 1938 Warner Bros. Pictures, Inc. Renewed 1965 by United Artists Television, Inc.

Page 63: From the United Artists release "POCKETFUL OF MIRACLES" © 1961 Franton Productions

Page 74 (left): From the Motion picture *The Coal Miner's Daughter" (Univ. 1980).* Courtesy of UNIVERSAL PICTURES

Page 74: (right): From the MGM release "A CHRISTMAS CAROL" © 1938 Loew's Inc. Renewed 1965 by Metro-Goldwyn Mayer Inc.

Page 75: From the MGM release "GONE WITH THE WIND" © 1939 Selznick International Pictures, Inc. Renewed 1967 by Metro-Goldwyn-Mayer Inc.

Page 82: From the United Artists release "MIDNIGHT COWBOY" © 1969 Jerome Hellman Productions, Inc.

Page 83: From "THE GOLD RUSH" (1925). Courtesy of Movie Star News.

Page 84: From "THE GRAPES OF WRATH". Copyright © 1940 TWENTIETH CENTURY-FOX FILM CORP. ALL RIGHTS RESERVED. COURTESY OF TWENTIETH CENTURY-FOX

Page 85 (top): From "IT'S A WONDERFUL LIFE" (1946). Courtesy of National Telefilm Associates, Inc., distributor, Los Angeles, CA.

Page 85 (bottom): From the United Artists release "HELL'S KITCHEN" © 1939 Warner Bros. Pictures, Inc. Renewed 1967 by United Artists Television, Inc.

Set in Times Roman by Leland & Penn, Inc., New York City